BACTERIA

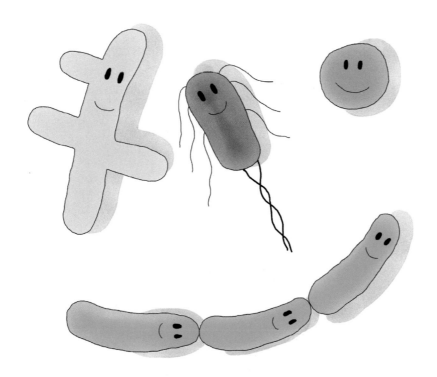

An Educational FunBook for Kids

(and Adults)

Idea, text, and illustrations: Alexander Matis

Go to

www.germtoons.com

for information about upcoming publications, products and
edutainment related to bacteria and other little critters.

Hi there! Have you ever heard of bacteria?

Possibly not — because you probably haven't ever seen any. Perhaps you've heard of them, but don't really know what they are. In any case, let me show you what bacteria are, and where to find them.

Look — there's a bacterium!

Can't you see it? That's because it's so small. How small? Hmm…

Let's start with a dog, because I'm sure you've seen lots of dogs in your life, and know how BIG or small they can be.

This is Nala. She's a small dog — a Pomeranian Spitz.

Oh — you'd better not ask me what that brown blot is! Bad dog, Nala!

But there is a fly right at the tip of the arrow. See how tiny it is!

Now, let's imagine we can zoom in, so the fly appears as big as Nala. Here we go!

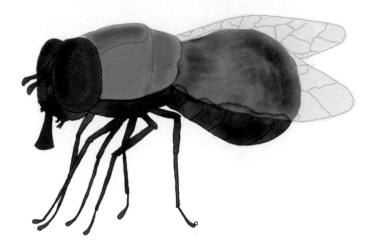

And now let's zoom in further, so the fly's leg looks as big as the whole fly did before.

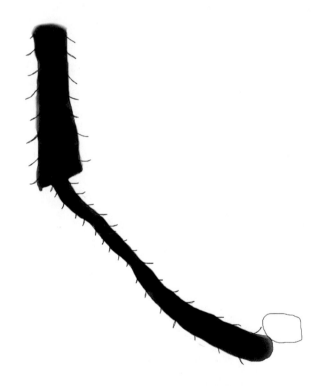

Look at that small white dot. That's a grain of powdered sugar.

The fly has just eaten some sugar.

Now let's imagine that we can magnify the sugar grain, so it looks as big as the fly did. Ah — do you see that speck?

That's a bacterium. Let's zoom in again, so we can look at it better.

Hello!

Usually, you would need a particular piece of equipment, called a microscope, to see individual bacteria.

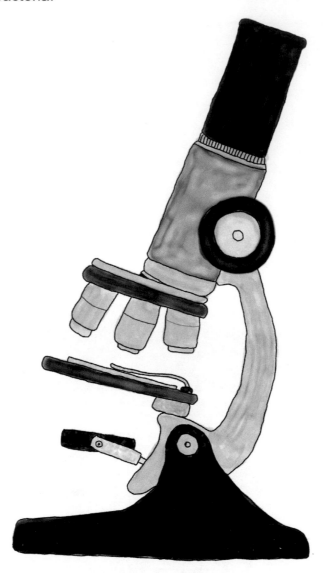

Under a microscope, bacteria might look like this.

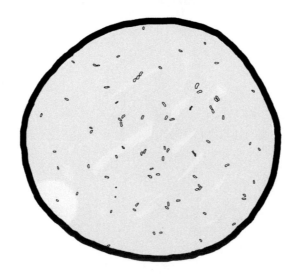

But to see them really close up, you need a special type of microscope, called an electron microscope.

This is what one of the same bacteria would look like under an electron microscope.

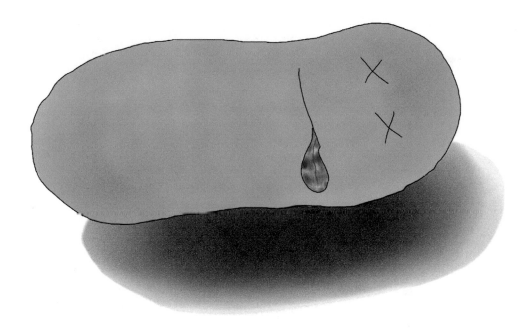

(Unfortunately, preparation for the electron microscope kills the bacteria)

Although they are extremely small, many types of bacteria play an essential role in your life, so it's absolutely worth getting to know them better.

So, what are bacteria?

They're not plants or animals.

They're not mushrooms.

In fact, they are a unique form of life.

Unlike us, who are built from many different building blocks, called cells, which commonly are connected to each other, a bacterium is built from just one cell.

And its insides are much simpler than the insides of most of our cells.

Most bacteria are also smaller than you people!

Bacteria come in many different shapes and forms. They can be round,

long,

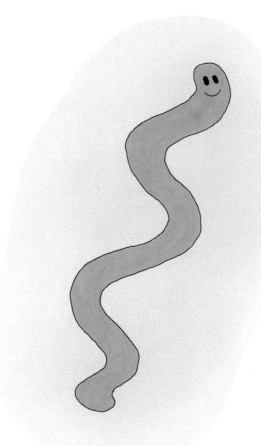

short,

"hairy",

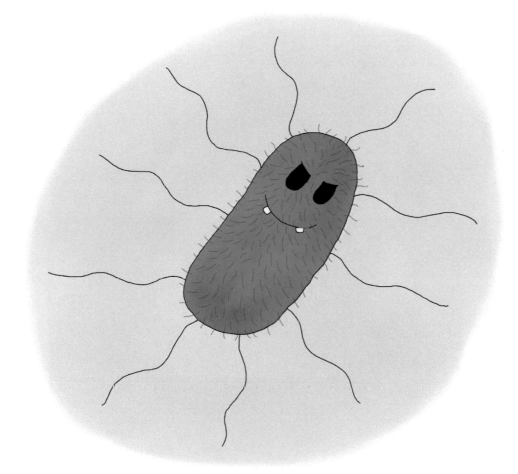

smooth,

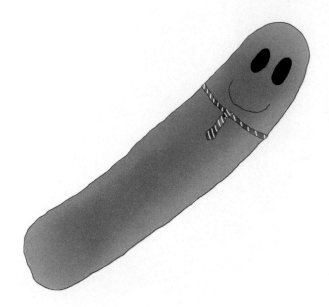

spiral,

straight,

or bent.

Some bacteria swim around very fast.

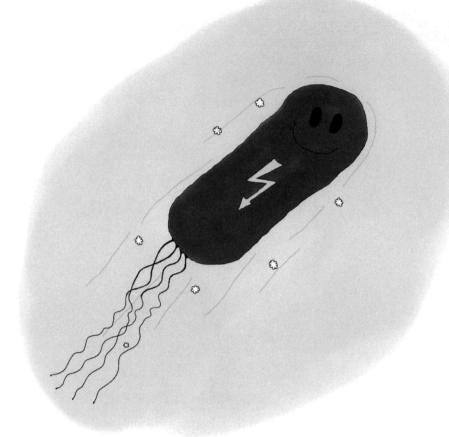

Others just stay where they are.

Some like to keep to themselves,

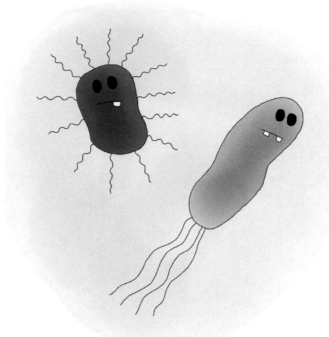

others prefer to stick together.

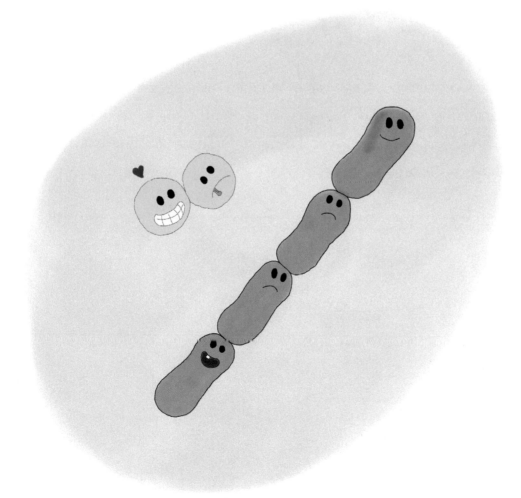

Bacteria increase their numbers by merely dividing themselves in two. So, if you start with one bacterium, pretty soon you'll have two bacteria, then four, then eight, and so on — you get the point.

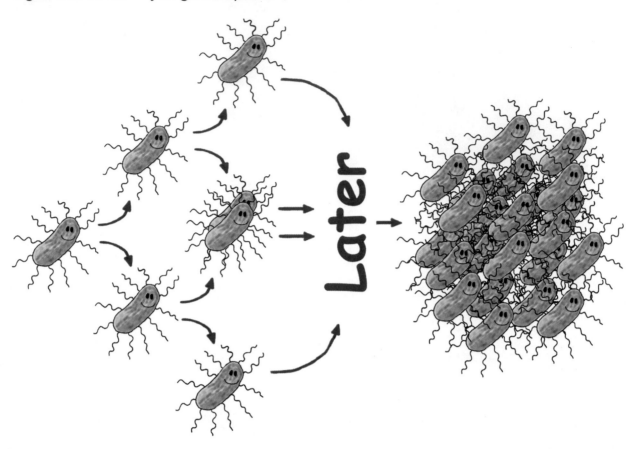

We can use this fact to make bacteria visible without a microscope. If you place one bacterium on some gel, with nutrients, in a Petri dish, it divides, and divides, and divides, and pretty soon, you'll be able to see a dot that contains millions of bacteria — a bacteria colony.

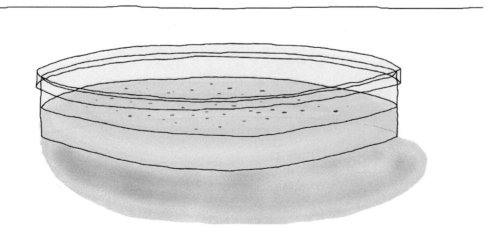

Some bacteria can divide themselves very fast. Under the right conditions in a laboratory, one bacterium, called *E. coli*, for example, can become two bacteria in just 15 minutes.

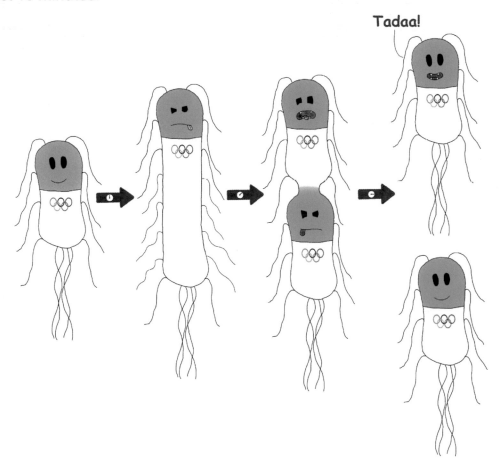

Others take much longer to divide into two — we are talking about hours or days here, so it's still pretty fast. Some bacteria can also fall into a sort of long sleep when the conditions they need to grow are bad — they become what are called spores.

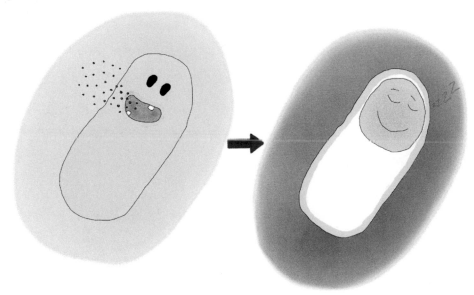

As spores, they are very well protected and can survive for years. They become active again only when the growing conditions improve.

Bacteria are almost everywhere — in the water, in the soil, in the air. Some bacteria are even on you, or in some parts of your body.

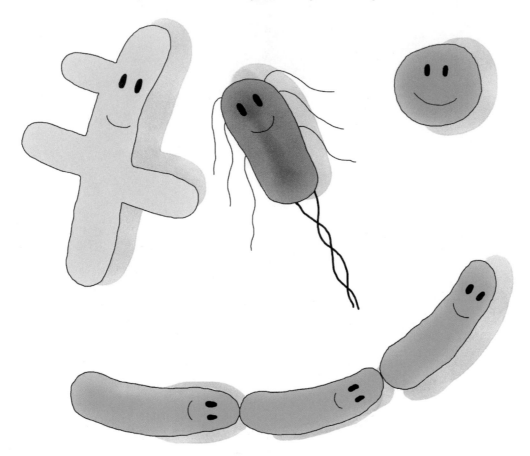

Nothing to be afraid of — we're nice bacteria!

In 2016 biologists at Indiana University have concluded that there are up to a trillion different kinds of bacteria living on Earth, most of which we have not yet discovered – that is more than 130 times the Earth's population. Four years earlier scientists at the University of Potsdam, Germany have estimated that about 2 nonillion bacteria are living on Earth.

That is far more than there are stars in the known universe!

Of course, you cannot really count such a large number of bacteria.

However, what you can do with some technical means is counting bacteria in defined spaces such as grains of sand. In 2017 German scientists from the town of Bremen did precisely that. They found that just one small grain of sand can be the home of up to 100,000 bacteria.

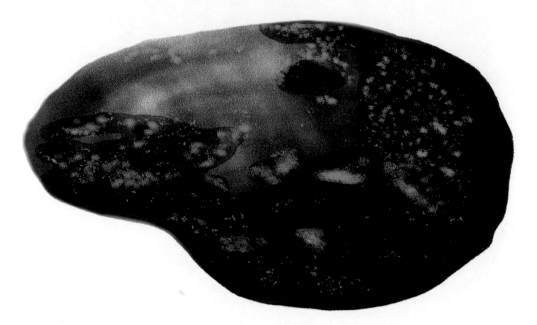

Here you can see a magnified typical grain of sand as examined by the scientists (actual size around 0.01 inches).
The bacteria were colored with green fluorescent dyes.

While there are so many of them, most bacteria happily live their lives without you even noticing them. But although you can't usually see them directly, others have a significant impact — good or bad — on your daily life.

Let's talk about the good bacteria first, because they outnumber the bad ones by far. Here's what the many different kinds of good bacteria do:

Good bacteria in water and soil eat up waste and chemicals, such as petrol, transforming poisonous substances into harmless materials over time. So they help nature to heal itself.

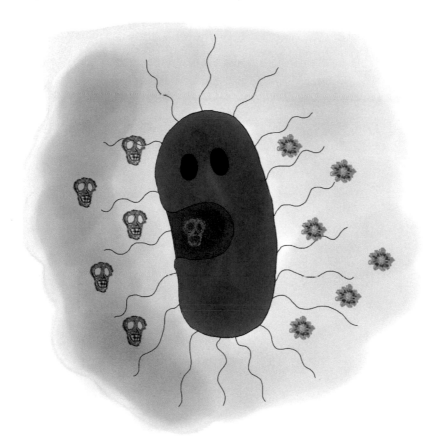

Bacteria also help break down organic matter, such as dead plants, leaves, and animals, and turn it into fertile soil. Without bacteria, there wouldn't be soil for plants to grow.

Some bacteria even create fertilizer for the plants they live with. Peas and beans, for example, depend on such bacteria, which provide them with specific fertilizer.

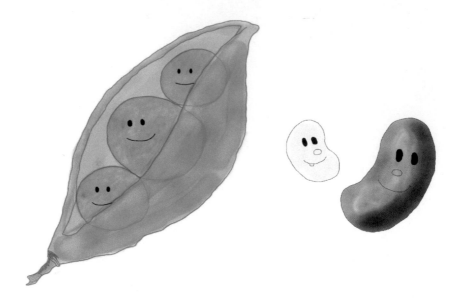

Other types of good bacteria help us make certain foods. Did you know that the following foods are made with the help of bacteria?

Sauerkraut,

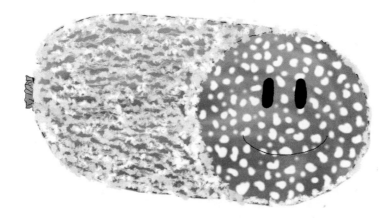

Salami,

yogurt,

various kinds of cheese,

23

vinegar, and...

ketchup

(And, honestly, could you survive without ketchup?)

Another bacterium we mentioned earlier, *E. coli*, can be transformed in a laboratory into a production machine for medicines and other helpful things.

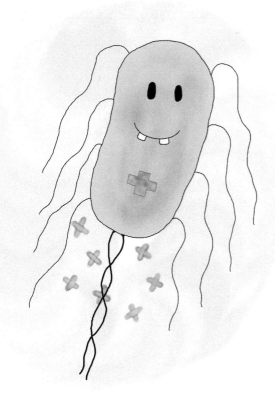

Also, bacteria living in your gut help you digest your food and produce healthy nutrients.

Finally, bacteria in your mouth and gut, and on your skin, even help you to stay healthy and fight off diseases, by preventing harmful bacteria from growing.

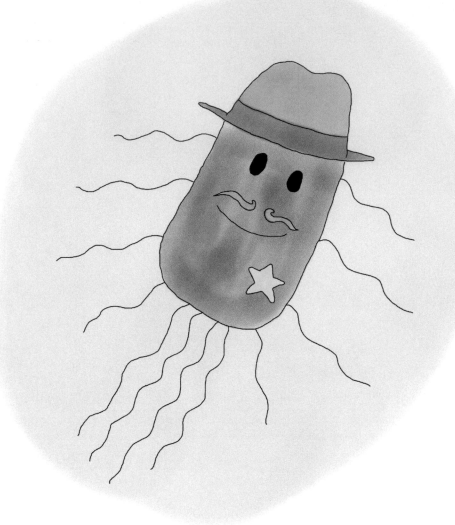

This brings us to the bad bacteria.

Bad bacteria can be spread via food and water, things you touch, and by other people, who have been infected by them previously.

Those little critters can make you smell bad. They can destroy your teeth. They can make you sick. On the following pages you are going to meet just some of them, but please don't be afraid….

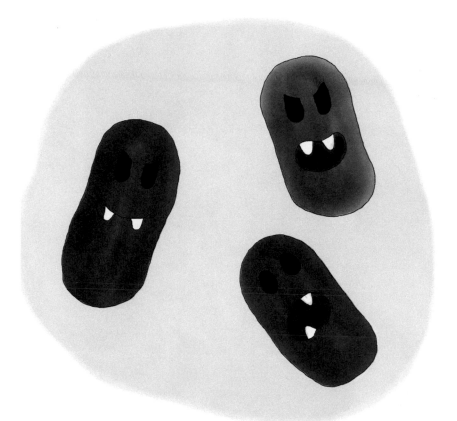

Corynebacterium jeikeium

We make smelly gases from your sweat.

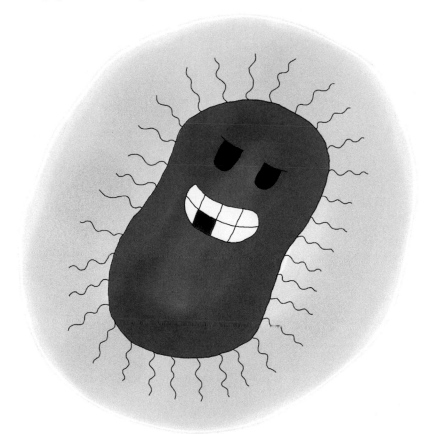

Porphyromonas gingivalis

I grow on your tongue and stink and taste bad.

Streptococcus mutans

We make acid out of the sugar you eat, which destroys your teeth.

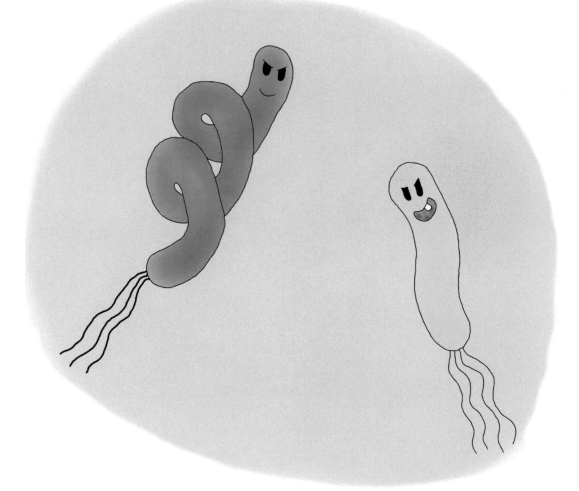

Campylobacter enteritis & Helicobacter pylori

We cause your belly to ache and make you vomit.

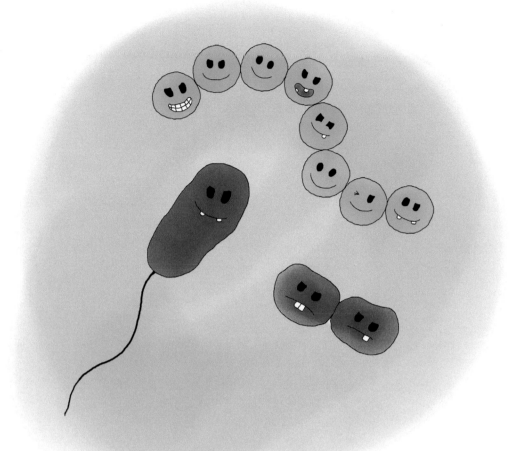

Legionella pneumophila, Streptococcus pyogenes, Moraxella catarrhalis

We make you cough and sneeze, and have a sore throat and ear pains.

Neisseria meningitides

We give you a headache.

That was scary, wasn't it?!

Luckily, you're not defenseless, and there are many ways to fight those baddies off and prevent them from harming you.

Firstly, your body has its own internal army of cells and tiny weapons, ready to fight off bacteria and other critters, and it's pretty good at that.

This defense mechanism is called your immune system.

And here's the good news:

You can train your immune system to be even better by letting yourself get dirty in sand or mud, playing with other kids, or stroking animals.

(So, next time you want to build a sandcastle with your friends or hold a cute bunny rabbit, tell your mum or dad that you need to do it to train your immune system.)

Another way to train your immune system specifically to fight off some of the worst bacteria is to get vaccinated against them.

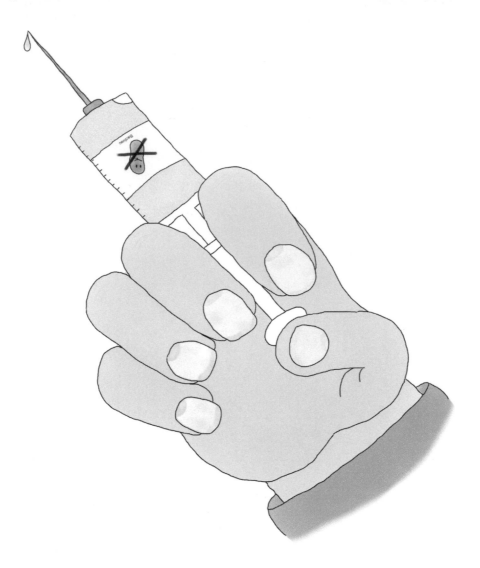

I know you don't want to be pricked by a needle, but believe me, it's better than having to fight against those critters without a trained immune system.

Secondly, you can help yourself and others to avoid being affected by bad bacteria by taking a few simple measures:

Brush your teeth regularly and thoroughly. If you can, also brush your tongue and, if you want to go one step further (and you should), you can use mouthwash, too.

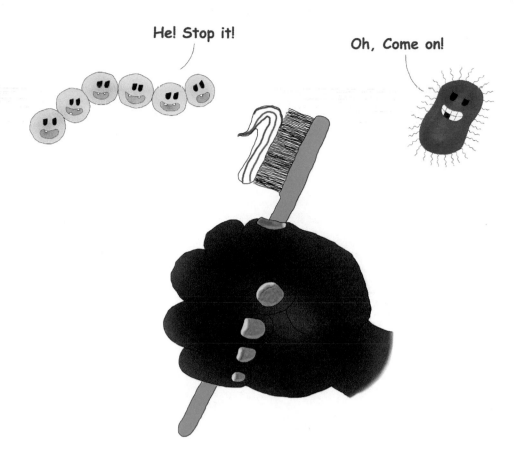

Wash your hands thoroughly whenever they are visibly dirty, after you've been to the toilet, and before you prepare food, or have a meal. Rub them against each other and use soap.

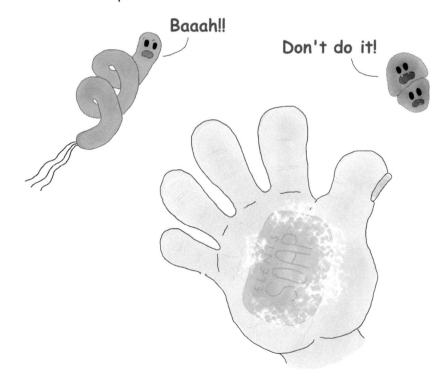

Take a bath or shower before you get smelly, or when you are grubby.

If you need to cough or sneeze, don't do it into your bare hand. It is best to sneeze into a paper tissue and to throw it away afterward. If you don't have a tissue at hand, sneeze into your elbow, or — if you are outside a building and not near any other people — sneeze on the ground.

If you forget and do sneeze into your hand, make sure you wash it afterward with soap. Imagine that: Scientists have discovered that some bacteria can spread up to 13 foot and remain alive in the air for up to 45 minutes after being coughed or sneezed.

Don't drink dirty water. If in doubt, it's better to drink bottled water. Don't eat food that tastes or smells bad.

If you are bleeding from a wound, don't let it get dirty and, if possible, treat it with disinfectant.

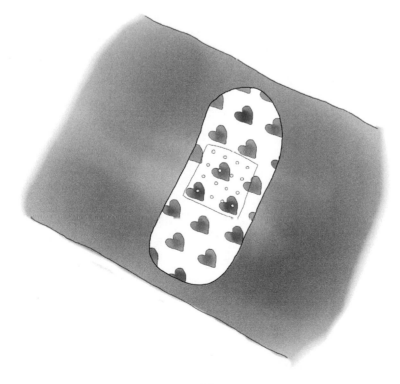

Finally, if you do get attacked by harmful bacteria, and your immune system can't handle them alone, your doctor can prescribe medicine — called antibiotics — that will help you deal with them effectively.

So, take care, but don't be afraid of bad bacteria. Rather be grateful for the many good bacteria in your life. And the next time you play outdoors, or when you eat peas, or yogurt, or ketchup, or when you…

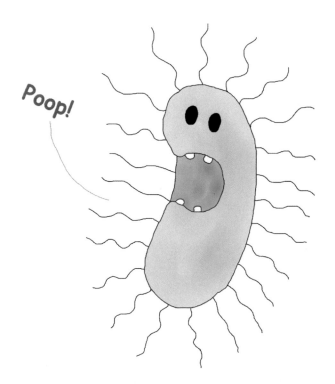

Just pause for a moment, and think about the tiny, tiny, tiny bacteria that you can't see, but make everything possible.

The End

Not yet. Let me tell you about…

The Real Bacteria

Of course, bacteria can't really talk, and they don't have eyes or mouths, as shown in this book.

Also, they are usually not very colorful when seen through a microscope, but we can color them in with dyes,

and fluorescence dyes.

However, bacteria colonies can be very colorful on a Petri dish.

Here you can see what bacteria actually look like:

On a Petri dish:

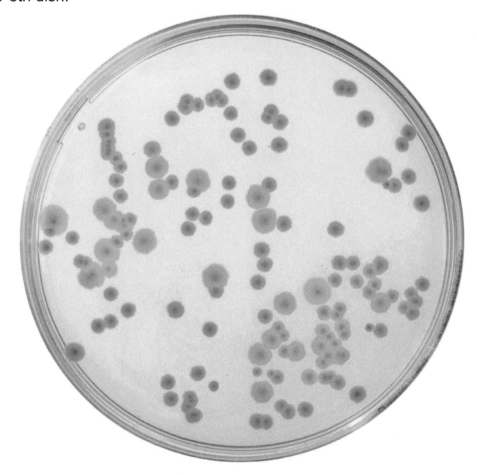

Under an optical microscope (after color-staining):

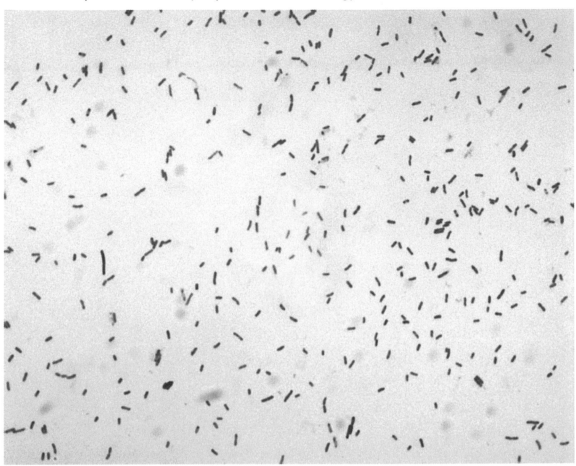

Under an electron microscope:

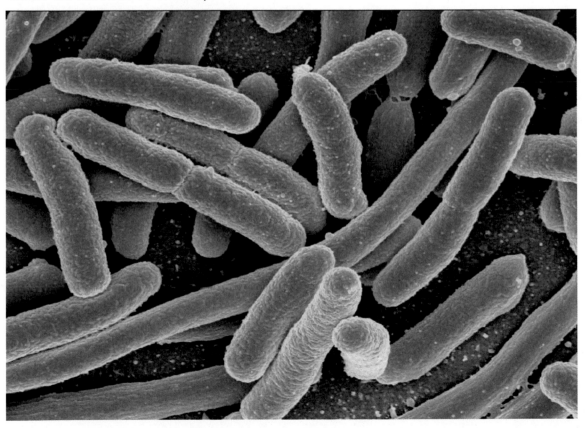

How to Grow Bacteria

Do you want to see bacteria with your own eyes on a Petri dish?
Here's a recipe for you:

Caution! For this experiment, you need to use boiling water. Hot water must only be handled by an adult.

Materials & equipment needed:

- 1 cup of water
- 1 teaspoon of agar or gelatin (gelatin may be easier to get, but can be liquefied by some bacteria)
- 1 teaspoon of sugar
- 1 teaspoon of beef- or chicken stock powder
- 1 microwavable glass- or plastic bowl
- Spoon
- 1 to 2 Petri dishes
- Sticky tape
- Felt-tip pen to label Petri dishes
- A warm place for incubation of the Petri dishes (e.g. under a lamp, near a heater, etc.)

How to proceed:

a. Pour the water into the bowl and bring to the boil in the microwave.
b. Add sugar, agar and meat stock powder to the boiling water and stir with spoon until all the ingredients have dissolved.
c. Cool the mixture for a couple of minutes. The mixture needs to be still liquid and hot.
d. Take the lids off the Petri dishes, but hold them as close above the Petri dishes as possible to avoid contamination. Have an adult quickly half-fill the Petri dishes with the hot mixture and immediately put the lids back on the Petri dishes. Do one Petri dish at a time. This should be done as fast as possible to avoid contamination with bacteria in the air.

e. Put the Petri dishes in the fridge for a couple of hours until the mixture has set and become solid. Once solid turn them upside down for storage. If you have worked properly, limiting contamination, you should be able to store the Petri dishes in the fridge for some days without unwanted growth of bacteria or fungi.

f. When you are ready to collect and grow your bacteria take the Petri dishes out of the fridge and expose them to bacteria (you may also catch some fungi). Here are some suggestions for gaining bacteria:

-   Gently print your fingers in the agar of the Petri dish;
-   Leave the Petri dish open for a couple of hours to expose it to the air;
-   Sprinkle some soil in a glass of water, mix and transfer some of the water with a cotton swab to the Petri dish;
-   Use a clean cotton swab to run it along various things and then rub it lightly across the agar of the Petri dish (you can e.g. do this with your skin, your mouth, the toilet seat, a computer keyboard, door handle, etc.

g. Put the lids back on the Petri dishes, turn them upside down and label them on the back with your felt-tip pen. Incubate the Petri dishes for 1 to 2 days in your incubator (warm place) or leave them at room temperature for up to 5 days. It is necessary to incubate the plates upside down to avoid condensation water from the lids dripping on the agar.

h. Observe every day. After a while you will start to see bacteria colonies or fungi that will grow bigger each day. If you want to slow down growth seal the Petri dishes with tape and put them back in the fridge. Keep them separated from food.

i. Once your experiment is finished, dispose the sealed Petri dishes in the bin.

For further information on how to grow bacteria and fungi and for ready-made kits to grow them visit our website (www.germtoons.com). There you can also have a peek at future publications of the book series.

Made in the USA
Coppell, TX
30 March 2022

75772012R00026